# 50 Delicious Spanish Dessert Recipes for Home

By: Kelly Johnson

# Table of Contents

- Tarta de Santiago (Almond Cake)
- Crema Catalana (Catalan Cream)
- Churros con Chocolate (Churros with Chocolate Sauce)
- Flan de Huevo (Spanish Custard Flan)
- Rosquillas (Spanish Doughnuts)
- Leche Frita (Fried Milk)
- Arroz con Leche (Spanish Rice Pudding)
- Polvorones (Spanish Shortbread Cookies)
- Bunyols de Quaresma (Lenten Doughnuts)
- Tocino de Cielo (Heaven's Bacon)
- Natillas (Spanish Custard)
- Torrijas (Spanish French Toast)
- Bizcocho de Naranja (Spanish Orange Cake)
- Mantecados (Spanish Crumbly Cookies)
- Bartolillos (Spanish Fried Pastries)
- Panellets (Almond Cookies)
- Pestiños (Honey Fritters)
- Crema de Limón (Lemon Cream)
- Polvorones de Almendra (Almond Shortbread)
- Suspiros de Monja (Nun's Sighs)
- Gachas Manchegas (Manchego Porridge)
- Buñuelos de Viento (Spanish Wind Fritters)
- Brazo de Gitano (Spanish Swiss Roll)
- Yemas de Santa Teresa (Saint Teresa's Yolks)
- Pestinos de Miel (Honey Cakes)
- Bollos de Aceite (Olive Oil Buns)
- Tarta de Queso (Spanish Cheesecake)
- Goxua (Basque Dessert)
- Croquetas de Chocolate (Chocolate Croquettes)
- Frutas de Aragón (Aragonese Fruits)
- Magdalenas (Spanish Muffins)
- Tejas (Spanish Lace Cookies)
- Cocas de San Juan (Saint John's Cakes)
- Mostachones de Utrera (Utrera Mustachios)
- Piononos (Andalusian Dessert)

- Mantecados de Cádiz (Cadiz Shortbread)
- Olla Podrida (Spanish Potpourri)
- Cuajada (Spanish Curd)
- Torrejas de Almendra (Almond Toast)
- Pestiños de Cádiz (Cadiz Honey Cakes)
- Torta de La Serena (La Serena Cheese Cake)
- Arrop i tallaetes (Valencian Molasses and Dough)
- Tarta de Manzana (Spanish Apple Tart)
- Melindres (Spanish Sweet Breadsticks)
- Mantecadas de Astorga (Astorga Shortbread)
- Fardelejos (Aragonese Pastries)
- Roscos de Anís (Aniseed Rings)
- Sobaos Pasiegos (Cantabrian Sponge Cakes)
- Tarta de Queso y Membrillo (Cheese and Quince Tart)
- Gató Mallorquín (Mallorcan Almond Cake)

**Tarta de Santiago (Almond Cake)**

Ingredients:

- 1 1/2 cups almond flour (ground almonds)
- 1 cup granulated sugar
- 4 large eggs
- Zest of 1 lemon
- 1 teaspoon almond extract (optional)
- Powdered sugar, for dusting
- Sliced almonds, for garnish (optional)

Instructions:

1. Preheat the Oven:
    - Preheat your oven to 350°F (175°C). Grease a 9-inch round cake pan and line the bottom with parchment paper.
2. Mix the Almond Flour and Sugar:
    - In a large mixing bowl, combine the almond flour and granulated sugar. Mix until well combined.
3. Add the Eggs and Flavorings:
    - Add the eggs to the almond flour mixture one at a time, beating well after each addition.
    - Stir in the lemon zest and almond extract (if using) until evenly incorporated into the batter.
4. Bake the Cake:
    - Pour the batter into the prepared cake pan and spread it out evenly.
    - Bake in the preheated oven for 25-30 minutes, or until the cake is golden brown and a toothpick inserted into the center comes out clean.
5. Cool and Garnish:
    - Allow the cake to cool in the pan for about 10 minutes, then transfer it to a wire rack to cool completely.
    - Once cooled, dust the top of the cake with powdered sugar.
    - Optionally, garnish the edges of the cake with sliced almonds for decoration.
6. Serve:
    - Slice the Tarta de Santiago into wedges and serve at room temperature.
    - Enjoy the rich almond flavor and tender texture of this classic Spanish dessert!

Tarta de Santiago is often enjoyed on its own as a sweet treat or served with a dollop of whipped cream or a scoop of vanilla ice cream for added indulgence. It's perfect for any occasion, from casual gatherings to special celebrations.

**Crema Catalana (Catalan Cream)**

Ingredients:

- 4 cups whole milk
- 6 large egg yolks
- 1 cup granulated sugar (divided)
- Zest of 1 lemon
- Zest of 1 orange
- 1 cinnamon stick
- 2 tablespoons cornstarch
- Extra granulated sugar for caramelizing

Instructions:

1. Prepare the Custard:
    - In a saucepan, heat the milk, lemon zest, orange zest, and cinnamon stick over medium heat until it begins to simmer. Do not let it boil.
    - In a mixing bowl, whisk together the egg yolks, cornstarch, and half of the sugar until smooth and pale yellow.
2. Temper the Eggs:
    - Slowly pour the hot milk mixture into the egg yolk mixture, whisking constantly to temper the eggs and prevent curdling.
3. Cook the Custard:
    - Return the mixture to the saucepan and cook over medium-low heat, stirring constantly with a wooden spoon or spatula, until the custard thickens enough to coat the back of the spoon. This usually takes about 8-10 minutes. Do not let it boil.
4. Strain the Custard:
    - Once the custard has thickened, remove it from the heat and strain it through a fine-mesh sieve into a clean bowl to remove the lemon zest, orange zest, and cinnamon stick.
5. Chill the Custard:
    - Cover the custard with plastic wrap, pressing it directly onto the surface to prevent a skin from forming.
    - Refrigerate the custard for at least 2 hours, or until thoroughly chilled and set.
6. Caramelize the Sugar:

- Just before serving, sprinkle a thin, even layer of granulated sugar over the surface of each custard-filled ramekin.
- Use a kitchen torch to caramelize the sugar until it forms a golden-brown crust. Alternatively, you can place the ramekins under a broiler for a few minutes until the sugar caramelizes.

7. Serve:
    - Allow the caramelized sugar to cool and harden for a minute or two before serving.
    - Serve the Crema Catalana immediately, garnished with fresh berries or a sprinkle of ground cinnamon if desired.

Enjoy the creamy richness and crunchy caramel topping of Crema Catalana, a delightful Spanish dessert perfect for any occasion!

# Churros con Chocolate (Churros with Chocolate Sauce)

Ingredients:

For the Churros:

- 1 cup water
- 2 tablespoons sugar
- 1/2 teaspoon salt
- 2 tablespoons vegetable oil
- 1 cup all-purpose flour
- Vegetable oil, for frying

For the Chocolate Sauce:

- 1 cup semisweet chocolate chips or chopped chocolate
- 1 cup heavy cream
- 1 teaspoon vanilla extract

Instructions:

1. Prepare the Chocolate Sauce:

   - In a small saucepan, heat the heavy cream over medium heat until it starts to simmer.
   - Place the chocolate chips or chopped chocolate in a heatproof bowl.
   - Pour the hot cream over the chocolate and let it sit for 1-2 minutes to soften the chocolate.
   - Add vanilla extract and stir the mixture until smooth and well combined. Set aside.

2. Make the Churro Dough:

   - In a medium saucepan, combine water, sugar, salt, and vegetable oil. Bring the mixture to a boil over medium heat.
   - Once boiling, remove the saucepan from the heat and add the flour all at once. Stir vigorously with a wooden spoon until the mixture forms a smooth dough and pulls away from the sides of the pan.

3. Fry the Churros:

- Heat vegetable oil in a large skillet or deep fryer to 375°F (190°C).
- Transfer the churro dough to a piping bag fitted with a large star tip.
- Pipe 4-6 inch long strips of dough directly into the hot oil, using scissors to cut the dough from the piping tip.
- Fry the churros in batches for 3-4 minutes, or until golden brown and crispy, flipping them halfway through cooking.
- Remove the fried churros from the oil using a slotted spoon and drain them on a paper towel-lined plate to remove excess oil.

4. Serve:

- Serve the warm churros immediately with the chocolate sauce for dipping.
- Optionally, dust the churros with powdered sugar or cinnamon sugar before serving for extra flavor.
- Enjoy the crispy exterior and tender interior of the churros dipped in the rich and velvety chocolate sauce!

Churros con Chocolate is a delightful treat perfect for breakfast, dessert, or anytime you crave something sweet and satisfying. Enjoy this classic Spanish delicacy with friends and family!

**Flan de Huevo (Spanish Custard Flan)**

Ingredients:

For the Caramel Sauce:

- 1 cup granulated sugar
- 1/4 cup water

For the Custard:

- 4 large eggs
- 1 can (14 ounces) sweetened condensed milk
- 1 can (12 ounces) evaporated milk
- 1 teaspoon vanilla extract

Instructions:

1. Prepare the Caramel Sauce:

    - In a small saucepan, combine the granulated sugar and water over medium heat.
    - Stir until the sugar is dissolved, then stop stirring and let the mixture come to a boil.
    - Cook without stirring until the sugar caramelizes and turns a golden amber color, swirling the pan occasionally to ensure even caramelization. Be careful not to burn the caramel.
    - Once the desired color is reached, immediately pour the caramel into the bottom of a 9-inch round cake pan or several individual ramekins, swirling to coat the bottom evenly. Work quickly as the caramel will harden fast.

2. Prepare the Custard Mixture:

    - Preheat your oven to 350°F (175°C).
    - In a large mixing bowl, whisk together the eggs, sweetened condensed milk, evaporated milk, and vanilla extract until smooth and well combined.

3. Pour the Custard Mixture:

    - Pour the custard mixture over the caramel layer in the cake pan or ramekins.

4. Bake the Flan:

- Place the cake pan or ramekins in a larger baking dish or roasting pan. Fill the larger dish with hot water until it reaches halfway up the sides of the cake pan or ramekins, creating a water bath.
- Carefully transfer the baking dish to the preheated oven and bake for 50-60 minutes, or until the custard is set around the edges but still slightly jiggly in the center.

5. Chill and Serve:

- Once baked, remove the flan from the oven and let it cool to room temperature.
- Refrigerate the flan for at least 4 hours, or preferably overnight, to allow it to fully set.

6. Unmold and Serve:

- To unmold the flan, run a knife around the edge of the cake pan or ramekins to loosen the edges.
- Place a serving plate upside down on top of the cake pan or ramekin and quickly invert it. The flan should release onto the plate with the caramel sauce on top.

7. Serve:

- Slice the flan into wedges or serve it in individual portions.
- Enjoy the creamy texture and caramel flavor of this classic Spanish dessert!

Flan de Huevo is best served chilled and can be enjoyed on its own or garnished with whipped cream, fresh fruit, or a sprinkle of cinnamon for extra flavor. It's a decadent and elegant dessert perfect for special occasions or any day of the week!

**Rosquillas (Spanish Doughnuts)**

Ingredients:

For the Dough:

- 2 cups all-purpose flour
- 1 teaspoon baking powder
- 1/4 teaspoon salt
- 1/2 cup granulated sugar
- 2 large eggs
- 1/4 cup milk
- 1/4 cup olive oil or vegetable oil
- Zest of 1 lemon or orange (optional)
- Oil for frying

For the Glaze (optional):

- 1 cup powdered sugar
- 2-3 tablespoons milk or water
- 1/2 teaspoon vanilla extract (optional)

Instructions:

1. Prepare the Dough:

    - In a large mixing bowl, whisk together the flour, baking powder, salt, and granulated sugar.
    - In a separate bowl, beat the eggs lightly, then add the milk, oil, and citrus zest (if using). Mix until well combined.
    - Gradually add the wet ingredients to the dry ingredients, stirring until a smooth dough forms. If the dough is too dry, add a little more milk as needed.

2. Shape the Dough:

    - On a lightly floured surface, roll out the dough to about 1/2 inch thickness.
    - Use a doughnut cutter or a round cookie cutter to cut out doughnut shapes. You can also shape the dough into rings by rolling it into ropes and pinching the ends together.

3. Fry the Rosquillas:

- In a deep saucepan or fryer, heat the oil to 350°F (175°C).
- Carefully place the doughnuts into the hot oil, a few at a time, making sure not to overcrowd the pan.
- Fry the doughnuts for 2-3 minutes per side, or until golden brown and cooked through.
- Use a slotted spoon or tongs to transfer the fried doughnuts to a paper towel-lined plate to drain off excess oil.

4. Make the Glaze (optional):

- In a small bowl, whisk together the powdered sugar, milk or water, and vanilla extract (if using) until smooth and well combined. Adjust the consistency by adding more milk or powdered sugar as needed.

5. Glaze the Rosquillas (optional):

- While the doughnuts are still warm, dip them into the glaze one at a time, coating them evenly.
- Place the glazed doughnuts on a wire rack set over a baking sheet to catch any drips. Allow the glaze to set for a few minutes before serving.

6. Serve:

- Serve the Rosquillas warm or at room temperature.
- Enjoy these delicious Spanish doughnuts with a cup of coffee or hot chocolate for a delightful treat!

Rosquillas are best enjoyed fresh on the day they are made, but they can be stored in an airtight container at room temperature for up to 2 days.

**Leche Frita (Fried Milk)**

Ingredients:

For the Custard:

- 4 cups whole milk
- 1 cinnamon stick
- Zest of 1 lemon
- Zest of 1 orange
- 1/2 cup granulated sugar
- 1/2 cup cornstarch
- 4 large egg yolks

For Coating and Frying:

- Vegetable oil, for frying
- 1 cup all-purpose flour
- 2 large eggs, beaten
- 1 cup fine breadcrumbs
- Granulated sugar, for dusting
- Ground cinnamon, for dusting

Instructions:

1. Prepare the Custard:

- In a large saucepan, combine the whole milk, cinnamon stick, lemon zest, and orange zest. Heat the mixture over medium heat until it comes to a simmer. Remove from heat and let it steep for 10-15 minutes to infuse the flavors.

2. Make the Custard Base:

- In a separate bowl, whisk together the granulated sugar, cornstarch, and egg yolks until smooth and well combined.
- Gradually pour the warm milk mixture into the egg mixture, whisking constantly to prevent curdling.

3. Cook the Custard:

- Return the combined mixture to the saucepan and place it over medium heat.
- Cook the custard, stirring constantly with a wooden spoon or spatula, until it thickens and coats the back of the spoon, about 5-7 minutes. Do not let it boil.

4. Set the Custard:

- Once the custard is thickened, remove it from the heat and pour it into a shallow dish or baking pan. Smooth the surface with a spatula.
- Let the custard cool to room temperature, then cover it with plastic wrap and refrigerate for at least 2 hours, or until firm and set.

5. Shape and Coat the Custard:

- Once the custard is chilled and firm, cut it into squares or rectangles of desired size.
- Set up three shallow bowls for coating: one with all-purpose flour, one with beaten eggs, and one with breadcrumbs.

6. Fry the Leche Frita:

- In a deep skillet or saucepan, heat vegetable oil over medium-high heat until it reaches 350°F (175°C).
- Dredge each piece of custard in the flour, then dip it into the beaten eggs, and finally coat it evenly with breadcrumbs.
- Fry the coated custard pieces in the hot oil until golden brown and crispy on all sides, about 2-3 minutes per side. Fry in batches to avoid overcrowding the pan.

7. Drain and Serve:

- Once fried, remove the Leche Frita from the oil using a slotted spoon and transfer them to a plate lined with paper towels to drain off excess oil.
- Dust the fried custard squares with a mixture of granulated sugar and ground cinnamon while still warm.
- Serve the Leche Frita immediately as a delicious and indulgent dessert.

Enjoy the crispy exterior and creamy interior of Leche Frita, a delightful Spanish treat that's perfect for any occasion!

**Arroz con Leche (Spanish Rice Pudding)**

Ingredients:

- 1 cup medium-grain rice (such as Arborio or Valencia)
- 4 cups whole milk
- 1/2 cup granulated sugar
- 1 cinnamon stick
- 1 teaspoon vanilla extract
- Zest of 1 lemon (optional)
- Ground cinnamon, for garnish

Instructions:

1. Rinse the Rice:

- Rinse the rice under cold water until the water runs clear. This helps remove excess starch and prevents the rice from becoming too sticky.

2. Cook the Rice:

- In a large saucepan, combine the rinsed rice, whole milk, cinnamon stick, and lemon zest (if using). Bring the mixture to a gentle simmer over medium heat, stirring occasionally to prevent the rice from sticking to the bottom of the pan.

3. Simmer and Stir:

- Once the mixture reaches a simmer, reduce the heat to low and let it cook uncovered, stirring frequently, for about 25-30 minutes, or until the rice is tender and the mixture has thickened to a creamy consistency.

4. Add Sugar and Flavorings:

- Stir in the granulated sugar and vanilla extract, continuing to cook for an additional 5-10 minutes until the sugar is fully dissolved and the flavors are well incorporated.

5. Serve:

- Remove the cinnamon stick from the rice pudding.
- Serve the Arroz con Leche warm or chilled, garnished with ground cinnamon on top for extra flavor.

6. Optional Garnishes:

- Arroz con Leche can be served plain or with additional toppings such as raisins, chopped nuts (such as almonds or walnuts), or a sprinkle of ground nutmeg.

7. Enjoy:

- Enjoy this comforting and delicious Spanish dessert as a sweet ending to any meal or as a comforting snack any time of day!

Arroz con Leche is a versatile dessert that can be enjoyed warm or cold, making it perfect for any occasion. Its creamy texture and fragrant spices are sure to delight your taste buds.

**Polvorones (Spanish Shortbread Cookies)**

Ingredients:

- 2 cups all-purpose flour
- 1 cup powdered sugar
- 1 cup unsalted butter, at room temperature
- 1/2 cup ground almonds or almond flour
- 1/2 teaspoon ground cinnamon (optional)
- 1/4 teaspoon ground cloves (optional)
- Pinch of salt
- Additional powdered sugar, for dusting

Instructions:

1. Preheat the Oven:

- Preheat your oven to 350°F (175°C) and line a baking sheet with parchment paper.

2. Toast the Almonds (if using whole almonds):

- If you're using whole almonds, spread them out on a baking sheet and toast them in the preheated oven for 8-10 minutes, or until lightly golden brown and fragrant. Let them cool completely, then grind them into a fine powder using a food processor or blender.

3. Mix the Dough:

- In a large mixing bowl, cream together the powdered sugar and softened butter until smooth and creamy.
- Add the ground almonds (or almond flour), flour, ground cinnamon, ground cloves, and a pinch of salt to the bowl. Mix until the dough comes together and forms a soft, crumbly texture.

4. Shape the Cookies:

- Take small portions of the dough and roll them into balls, about 1 inch in diameter. Place the balls onto the prepared baking sheet, spacing them slightly apart.

5. Flatten and Decorate:

- Use the bottom of a glass or the palm of your hand to gently flatten each dough ball into a thick disc, about 1/2 inch thick.
- Optionally, you can use a cookie stamp or the tines of a fork to create decorative patterns on the surface of the cookies.

6. Bake:

- Bake the Polvorones in the preheated oven for 12-15 minutes, or until the edges are lightly golden brown.

7. Cool and Dust:

- Remove the cookies from the oven and let them cool on the baking sheet for a few minutes before transferring them to a wire rack to cool completely.
- Once cooled, dust the Polvorones with powdered sugar while still slightly warm.

8. Serve and Enjoy:

- Serve the Polvorones with a cup of coffee or tea, and enjoy their crumbly texture and buttery flavor!

These Polvorones can be stored in an airtight container at room temperature for up to one week. They make a delightful treat for any occasion and are sure to be a hit with family and friends!

**Bunyols de Quaresma (Lenten Doughnuts)**

Ingredients:

- 1 cup water
- 1/4 cup vegetable oil (plus more for frying)
- 1/4 teaspoon salt
- 1 cup all-purpose flour
- 1/4 cup granulated sugar
- 1 teaspoon ground cinnamon
- Zest of 1 lemon (optional)
- Powdered sugar, for dusting (optional)

Instructions:

1. Prepare the Dough:

   - In a saucepan, bring the water, vegetable oil, and salt to a boil over medium heat.

2. Add the Flour:

   - Once the mixture comes to a boil, remove it from the heat and immediately stir in the flour until well combined and a smooth dough forms.

3. Let the Dough Rest:

   - Transfer the dough to a mixing bowl and let it cool for a few minutes.

4. Mix the Sugar and Cinnamon:

   - In a shallow dish, mix together the granulated sugar, ground cinnamon, and lemon zest (if using). This will be used for coating the doughnuts later.

5. Heat the Oil:

   - In a deep fryer or heavy-bottomed pot, heat vegetable oil to 350°F (175°C).

6. Shape and Fry the Doughnuts:

- Scoop up small portions of the dough and shape them into balls, about 1 inch in diameter.
- Carefully drop the dough balls into the hot oil, frying them in batches to avoid overcrowding the pot.
- Fry the doughnuts for 3-4 minutes, or until they are golden brown and cooked through, turning them occasionally for even browning.

7. Coat the Doughnuts:

- Once the doughnuts are cooked, remove them from the oil using a slotted spoon and drain them on paper towels to remove excess oil.
- While the doughnuts are still warm, roll them in the cinnamon-sugar mixture until they are evenly coated.

8. Serve:

- Transfer the coated Bunyols de Quaresma to a serving platter and sprinkle them with powdered sugar if desired.
- Enjoy these delightful Lenten doughnuts as a sweet treat during the Lenten season!

Bunyols de Quaresma are best enjoyed fresh and warm, but they can also be stored in an airtight container at room temperature for up to two days.

**Tocino de Cielo (Heaven's Bacon)**

Ingredients:

- 12 egg yolks
- 1 cup granulated sugar
- 1/2 cup water
- Caramel sauce (optional, for serving)

Instructions:

1. Preheat the Oven:

- Preheat your oven to 350°F (175°C). Place a larger baking dish filled with water on the bottom rack of the oven. This will create a water bath for baking the Tocino de Cielo and help prevent it from cracking.

2. Prepare the Caramel:

- If you're not using pre-made caramel sauce, you can make caramel by melting sugar in a saucepan over medium heat until it turns into a golden-brown syrup. Pour the caramel into the bottom of individual ramekins or a large baking dish, swirling to coat the bottom evenly. Let it cool and harden.

3. Make the Custard:

- In a large mixing bowl, whisk together the egg yolks until smooth and well combined.

4. Prepare the Sugar Syrup:

- In a saucepan, combine the granulated sugar and water. Heat over medium heat, stirring constantly, until the sugar is completely dissolved and the mixture becomes syrupy. Remove from heat and let it cool slightly.

5. Combine the Ingredients:

- Slowly pour the sugar syrup into the beaten egg yolks, whisking continuously to prevent the eggs from scrambling. Make sure the syrup has cooled slightly to avoid cooking the eggs.

6. Strain the Mixture:

- Strain the egg and sugar mixture through a fine-mesh sieve to remove any lumps or impurities. This step ensures a smooth and creamy texture for the Tocino de Cielo.

7. Fill the Ramekins:

- Pour the strained custard mixture into the prepared ramekins or baking dish with caramel sauce, filling them almost to the top.

8. Bake the Tocino de Cielo:

- Place the filled ramekins or baking dish in the oven, inside the larger dish with water. Bake for about 25-30 minutes, or until the custard is set but still jiggly in the center.

9. Chill and Serve:

- Remove the Tocino de Cielo from the oven and let it cool to room temperature. Then, transfer it to the refrigerator to chill for at least 2 hours or until completely set.
- Once chilled, run a knife around the edges of the ramekins to loosen the custard. Invert the ramekins onto serving plates to release the Tocino de Cielo. If using a large baking dish, you can slice and serve directly from the dish.
- Optionally, drizzle with additional caramel sauce before serving.

10. Enjoy:

- Serve the Tocino de Cielo chilled and enjoy its rich, creamy texture and sweet caramel flavor.

Tocino de Cielo is a decadent and indulgent dessert that is sure to impress your guests with its heavenly taste and appearance.

## Natillas (Spanish Custard)

Ingredients:

- 4 cups whole milk
- 6 large egg yolks
- 1 cup granulated sugar
- 1/4 cup cornstarch
- 1 cinnamon stick
- Zest of 1 lemon
- Ground cinnamon, for garnish

Instructions:

1. Heat the Milk:

- In a saucepan, heat the whole milk over medium heat until it comes to a gentle simmer. Add the cinnamon stick and lemon zest, then reduce the heat to low and let it infuse for about 5 minutes. Remove from heat and discard the cinnamon stick.

2. Prepare the Egg Mixture:

- In a mixing bowl, whisk together the egg yolks, granulated sugar, and cornstarch until well combined and smooth.

3. Temper the Eggs:

- Gradually pour a small amount of the warm milk into the egg mixture while whisking continuously. This process, known as tempering, prevents the eggs from curdling when added to the hot milk.

4. Combine the Mixtures:

- Once tempered, pour the egg mixture back into the saucepan with the remaining warm milk, whisking constantly to combine.

5. Cook the Custard:

- Place the saucepan back over medium heat and cook the custard mixture, stirring constantly with a wooden spoon or spatula, until it thickens and coats the back of the spoon, about 8-10 minutes. Be careful not to let it boil.

6. Strain the Custard:

- Once the custard has thickened, remove it from the heat and strain it through a fine-mesh sieve to remove any lumps or impurities. This step ensures a smooth and creamy texture for the Natillas.

7. Chill:

- Transfer the strained custard into individual serving dishes or a large bowl. Cover with plastic wrap, pressing it directly onto the surface of the custard to prevent a skin from forming. Chill in the refrigerator for at least 2 hours, or until completely cold and set.

8. Serve:

- Once chilled, remove the Natillas from the refrigerator and sprinkle with ground cinnamon for garnish.
- Serve the Natillas cold as a refreshing and creamy dessert.

Natillas can be stored in the refrigerator for up to 3 days. Enjoy this classic Spanish custard on its own or with a sprinkle of cinnamon for a delightful treat!

**Torrijas (Spanish French Toast)**

Ingredients:

- 1 loaf of day-old bread (such as French bread or baguette), sliced into thick slices
- 4 cups whole milk
- 1 cup granulated sugar, plus extra for coating
- 1 cinnamon stick
- Peel of 1 lemon or orange
- 4 large eggs
- Vegetable oil, for frying
- Ground cinnamon, for dusting

Instructions:

1. Prepare the Milk Mixture:

- In a saucepan, combine the whole milk, granulated sugar, cinnamon stick, and citrus peel. Heat the mixture over medium heat until it comes to a simmer. Remove from heat and let it cool slightly.

2. Soak the Bread:

- Place the sliced bread in a shallow dish or baking dish large enough to hold them in a single layer.
- Pour the warm milk mixture over the bread slices, making sure they are completely submerged. Let them soak for about 10-15 minutes, turning them halfway through, until they have absorbed the liquid.

3. Dip in Egg Mixture:

- In a separate shallow dish, beat the eggs until well combined.
- Carefully lift each soaked bread slice from the milk mixture and dip it into the beaten eggs, coating both sides evenly.

4. Fry the Torrijas:

- In a large skillet or frying pan, heat vegetable oil over medium heat until hot but not smoking.

- Working in batches, carefully place the dipped bread slices into the hot oil and fry until golden brown and crispy on both sides, about 2-3 minutes per side. Use a spatula to flip them halfway through cooking.

5. Drain and Coat:

- Once golden brown, remove the fried Torrijas from the oil and transfer them to a plate lined with paper towels to drain off any excess oil.
- While still warm, coat the Torrijas generously with granulated sugar mixed with ground cinnamon, shaking off any excess.

6. Serve:

- Serve the Torrijas warm or at room temperature as a delicious and comforting dessert.
- Optionally, you can drizzle them with honey or syrup before serving for extra sweetness.

Enjoy these delightful Spanish French toast treats as a special indulgence during Lent and Easter, or anytime you crave a sweet and comforting dessert!

Bizcocho de Naranja (Spanish Orange Cake)

## Ingredients:

- 1 1/2 cups all-purpose flour
- 1 1/2 teaspoons baking powder
- 1/4 teaspoon salt
- 1 cup granulated sugar
- 3 large eggs
- 1/2 cup vegetable oil
- 1/2 cup fresh orange juice
- Zest of 1 orange
- 1 teaspoon vanilla extract

## Instructions:

1. Preheat the Oven:

   - Preheat your oven to 350°F (175°C). Grease and flour a 9-inch round cake pan or line it with parchment paper for easy removal.

2. Mix Dry Ingredients:

   - In a mixing bowl, sift together the all-purpose flour, baking powder, and salt. Set aside.

3. Beat Sugar and Eggs:

   - In a separate mixing bowl, beat the granulated sugar and eggs together using a handheld mixer or stand mixer until pale and fluffy.

4. Add Wet Ingredients:

   - Gradually add the vegetable oil, fresh orange juice, orange zest, and vanilla extract to the sugar and egg mixture, beating until well combined.

5. Combine Dry and Wet Ingredients:

   - Gradually add the dry ingredients to the wet ingredients, mixing until just combined. Be careful not to overmix, as this can result in a dense cake.

6. Pour Batter into Pan:

   - Pour the batter into the prepared cake pan, spreading it evenly with a spatula.

7. Bake:

   - Bake the Bizcocho de Naranja in the preheated oven for 30-35 minutes, or until a toothpick inserted into the center comes out clean.

8. Cool and Serve:

   - Allow the cake to cool in the pan for 10 minutes, then transfer it to a wire rack to cool completely.
   - Once cooled, slice and serve the Bizcocho de Naranja on its own or with a dusting of powdered sugar or a dollop of whipped cream for added sweetness.

9. Store:

- Store any leftover cake in an airtight container at room temperature for up to 3 days, or in the refrigerator for longer freshness.

Enjoy the bright and citrusy flavors of this delightful Spanish Orange Cake with a cup of tea or coffee for a perfect afternoon treat or dessert!

**Mantecados (Spanish Crumbly Cookies)**

Ingredients:

- 2 cups all-purpose flour
- 1 cup powdered sugar
- 1 cup lard (or vegetable shortening), at room temperature
- 1/4 teaspoon ground cinnamon (optional)
- Zest of 1 lemon (optional)
- Pinch of salt

Instructions:

1. Preheat the Oven:

- Preheat your oven to 350°F (175°C). Line a baking sheet with parchment paper or silicone baking mat.

2. Mix Dry Ingredients:

- In a mixing bowl, sift together the all-purpose flour, powdered sugar, ground cinnamon (if using), and a pinch of salt. Add the lemon zest (if using) and mix until well combined.

3. Incorporate the Lard:

- Add the lard (or vegetable shortening) to the dry ingredients. Using your hands or a pastry cutter, work the lard into the flour mixture until it resembles coarse crumbs and holds together when pressed.

4. Form the Cookies:

- Take small portions of the dough and shape them into balls, about 1 inch in diameter. Place the balls onto the prepared baking sheet, spacing them slightly apart.

5. Flatten:

- Use the bottom of a glass or the palm of your hand to gently flatten each dough ball into a thick disc, about 1/2 inch thick.

6. Score:

    - Use a sharp knife to score a crisscross pattern on the top of each cookie. This not only adds visual appeal but also helps the cookies bake evenly.

7. Bake:

    - Bake the Mantecados in the preheated oven for 12-15 minutes, or until they are lightly golden brown around the edges.

8. Cool:

    - Remove the cookies from the oven and let them cool on the baking sheet for a few minutes before transferring them to a wire rack to cool completely.

9. Serve:

    - Once cooled, serve the Mantecados with a cup of coffee or hot chocolate for a delightful treat. They can also be enjoyed on their own as a snack or dessert.

10. Store:

    - Store the Mantecados in an airtight container at room temperature for up to one week. They also freeze well for longer storage.

Enjoy these traditional Spanish Mantecados as a delicious and crumbly addition to your holiday festivities or any time you crave a buttery treat!

**Bartolillos (Spanish Fried Pastries)**

Ingredients:

For the Dough:

- 2 cups all-purpose flour
- 1/4 cup granulated sugar
- 1/4 teaspoon salt
- 1/2 cup unsalted butter, cold and cubed
- 1 large egg
- 2-3 tablespoons cold water

For the Filling:

- 2 cups milk
- 1/2 cup granulated sugar
- 4 large egg yolks
- 1/4 cup cornstarch
- 1 teaspoon vanilla extract
- Zest of 1 lemon or orange (optional)
- Jam or fruit preserves of your choice (optional)

For Frying:

- Vegetable oil, for frying

For Dusting:

- Powdered sugar

Instructions:

1. Make the Dough:

- In a large mixing bowl, combine the all-purpose flour, granulated sugar, and salt. Add the cubed unsalted butter and rub it into the flour mixture using your fingertips until it resembles coarse crumbs.
- Add the egg and 2 tablespoons of cold water to the mixture. Stir until the dough comes together, adding more water if necessary. Knead the dough gently until smooth. Wrap it in plastic wrap and refrigerate for at least 30 minutes.

2. Prepare the Filling:

- In a saucepan, heat the milk until it just begins to simmer. In a separate bowl, whisk together the granulated sugar, egg yolks, and cornstarch until smooth and well combined.
- Slowly pour the hot milk into the egg mixture, whisking constantly to prevent curdling. Return the mixture to the saucepan and cook over medium heat, stirring constantly, until thickened.
- Remove the custard from the heat and stir in the vanilla extract and lemon or orange zest (if using). Let the custard cool completely.

3. Roll Out the Dough:

- On a lightly floured surface, roll out the chilled dough to about 1/8 inch thickness. Use a round cutter or glass to cut out circles of dough, about 3-4 inches in diameter.

4. Fill and Fold:

- Place a small spoonful of custard or fruit jam in the center of each dough circle. Fold the dough over to enclose the filling, forming a half-moon shape. Press the edges firmly to seal.

5. Fry the Bartolillos:

- In a deep fryer or large pot, heat vegetable oil to 350°F (175°C). Carefully add the filled Bartolillos to the hot oil in batches, frying until golden brown on both sides, about 2-3 minutes per side. Remove with a slotted spoon and drain on paper towels.

6. Dust and Serve:

- Once fried, dust the Bartolillos with powdered sugar while still warm. Serve them immediately as a delicious sweet treat.

7. Enjoy:

- Enjoy your homemade Bartolillos with a cup of coffee or tea for a delightful Spanish dessert experience!

These Bartolillos can be stored in an airtight container at room temperature for up to two days, but they are best enjoyed fresh and warm.

**Panellets (Almond Cookies)**

Ingredients:

- 2 cups ground almonds
- 1 cup granulated sugar
- Zest of 1 lemon
- 1 large egg
- 1 teaspoon vanilla extract
- Pine nuts (for topping)
- Powdered sugar (for coating, optional)

Instructions:

1. Preheat the Oven:

- Preheat your oven to 350°F (175°C). Line a baking sheet with parchment paper.

2. Prepare the Dough:

- In a mixing bowl, combine the ground almonds, granulated sugar, and lemon zest. Mix well.
- Add the egg and vanilla extract to the dry ingredients. Mix until a dough forms. If the dough is too dry, you can add a little water, one tablespoon at a time, until it comes together.

3. Shape the Panellets:

- Pinch off small pieces of dough and roll them into small balls, about 1 inch in diameter.
- Roll each ball in pine nuts, pressing lightly to adhere the nuts to the dough.
- Place the coated balls on the prepared baking sheet, spacing them slightly apart.

4. Bake:

- Bake the Panellets in the preheated oven for 12-15 minutes, or until they are lightly golden brown.

5. Optional Coating:

- If desired, while the Panellets are still warm, roll them in powdered sugar to coat. This step adds extra sweetness and a decorative touch.

6. Cool and Serve:

- Let the Panellets cool on the baking sheet for a few minutes before transferring them to a wire rack to cool completely.
- Once cooled, serve the Panellets as a delightful sweet treat for All Saints' Day or any special occasion.

7. Storage:

- Store any leftover Panellets in an airtight container at room temperature for up to one week.

Enjoy these traditional Catalan almond cookies as a delicious and festive addition to your holiday celebrations!

**Pestiños (Honey Fritters)**

Ingredients:

- 4 cups (500g) all-purpose flour
- 1 teaspoon ground cinnamon
- 1 teaspoon ground anise seeds (optional)
- Pinch of salt
- 1 cup (240ml) dry white wine
- 1 cup (240ml) olive oil
- Vegetable oil for frying
- Honey for dipping

Instructions:

1. Prepare the Dough:
    - In a large mixing bowl, combine the flour, cinnamon, anise seeds (if using), and salt.
    - Make a well in the center of the flour mixture and pour in the wine and olive oil.
    - Gradually incorporate the dry ingredients into the wet ingredients until a dough forms. If the dough is too dry, you can add a little more wine.
    - Knead the dough on a lightly floured surface until smooth. Cover it with a clean kitchen towel and let it rest for about 30 minutes.
2. Shape the Pestiños:
    - After the dough has rested, divide it into small portions and roll each portion into a thin rectangle, about 1/8 inch thick.
    - Cut the rectangles into diamond shapes or rectangles, whichever you prefer. You can use a pastry cutter or a knife for this.
3. Fry the Pestiños:
    - Heat vegetable oil in a deep frying pan or pot over medium heat.
    - Once the oil is hot, carefully add the pestiños in batches, frying them until they are golden brown on both sides. This usually takes about 2-3 minutes per side.
    - Remove the fried pestiños with a slotted spoon and place them on a plate lined with paper towels to drain any excess oil.
4. Coat with Honey:
    - While the pestiños are still warm, dip them in a bowl of honey, making sure they are fully coated.

- Place the honey-coated pestiños on a wire rack to allow any excess honey to drip off.
5. Serve:
    - Once the pestiños have cooled slightly and the excess honey has dripped off, they are ready to serve. Enjoy them as a sweet treat with a cup of coffee or tea!

Pestiños are best enjoyed fresh but can be stored in an airtight container for a few days.

Just be sure to reheat them briefly in the oven before serving to restore their crispiness.

**Crema de Limón (Lemon Cream)**

Ingredients:

- 4 large lemons (for zest and juice)
- 1 cup (200g) granulated sugar
- 4 large eggs
- 1/2 cup (115g) unsalted butter, softened
- Whipped cream and lemon zest (for garnish, optional)

Instructions:

1. Prepare Lemon Zest and Juice:
    - Wash the lemons thoroughly to remove any dirt or wax. Using a zester or a fine grater, zest the lemons to obtain about 2 tablespoons of zest. Set aside.
    - Juice the lemons to get about 3/4 cup (180ml) of fresh lemon juice. Set aside.
2. Prepare Double Boiler:
    - Fill a saucepan with a few inches of water and bring it to a simmer over medium heat. Place a heatproof bowl on top of the saucepan, ensuring that the bottom of the bowl doesn't touch the water. This setup creates a double boiler.
3. Combine Ingredients:
    - In the heatproof bowl, whisk together the granulated sugar, lemon zest, lemon juice, and eggs until well combined.
4. Cook the Lemon Mixture:
    - Place the bowl over the simmering water in the saucepan, making sure the water doesn't touch the bottom of the bowl.
    - Cook the lemon mixture, whisking constantly, until it thickens to a custard-like consistency. This usually takes about 10-15 minutes.
5. Incorporate Butter:
    - Once the mixture has thickened, remove the bowl from the heat. Cut the softened butter into small pieces and add them to the lemon mixture, stirring until the butter is completely melted and incorporated.
6. Chill and Serve:
    - Transfer the lemon cream to a clean bowl or individual serving dishes.
    - Cover the surface of the lemon cream with plastic wrap to prevent a skin from forming.

- Refrigerate the lemon cream for at least 2 hours, or until it's well chilled and set.
7. Garnish and Serve:
    - Before serving, you can garnish the lemon cream with a dollop of whipped cream and a sprinkle of lemon zest for an extra touch of freshness and flavor.
    - Serve chilled and enjoy the creamy, lemony goodness!

Crema de Limón is a versatile dessert that can be served on its own or as a topping for cakes, tarts, or fruit salads. Its vibrant flavor and creamy texture make it a delightful treat for lemon lovers.

**Polvorones de Almendra (Almond Shortbread)**

Ingredients:

- 2 cups (240g) all-purpose flour
- 1 cup (120g) almond flour (ground almonds)
- 1 cup (225g) unsalted butter, softened
- 1 cup (100g) powdered sugar
- 1 teaspoon ground cinnamon
- 1/2 teaspoon almond extract
- Whole almonds for decoration (optional)

Instructions:

1. Preheat the Oven:
    - Preheat your oven to 350°F (175°C). Line a baking sheet with parchment paper or silicone baking mats.
2. Prepare the Dough:
    - In a mixing bowl, combine the all-purpose flour, almond flour, powdered sugar, and ground cinnamon.
    - Add the softened butter and almond extract to the dry ingredients.
    - Using your hands or a mixer, mix the ingredients until a soft dough forms. Be careful not to overmix.
3. Shape the Cookies:
    - Take small portions of the dough and roll them into balls, each about 1 inch (2.5 cm) in diameter.
    - Place the dough balls on the prepared baking sheet, leaving some space between them.
4. Press and Decorate:
    - Use the bottom of a glass or your fingers to gently press down on each dough ball to flatten it into a disc shape. If desired, press a whole almond into the center of each cookie for decoration.
5. Bake:
    - Place the baking sheet in the preheated oven and bake the cookies for about 12-15 minutes, or until they are just beginning to turn golden around the edges. Be careful not to overbake them.
6. Cool:
    - Once baked, remove the cookies from the oven and let them cool on the baking sheet for a few minutes.

- Transfer the cookies to a wire rack to cool completely. They will continue to firm up as they cool.
7. Serve and Enjoy:
    - Once the cookies have cooled completely, they are ready to be enjoyed! Serve them with a cup of coffee or tea, or package them up in a pretty tin to give as gifts during the holidays.

These Polvorones de Almendra have a delightful crumbly texture and a rich almond flavor that's sure to please. They can be stored in an airtight container at room temperature for several days, making them a perfect make-ahead treat for any occasion. Enjoy!

**Suspiros de Monja (Nun's Sighs)**

Ingredients:

- 4 large eggs, separated
- 1 cup (200g) granulated sugar
- 1/4 teaspoon cream of tartar
- Pinch of salt
- Powdered sugar, for dusting

Instructions:

1. Preheat the Oven:
    - Preheat your oven to 325°F (160°C). Line a baking sheet with parchment paper or a silicone baking mat.
2. Prepare Egg Whites:
    - In a clean, dry mixing bowl, beat the egg whites with an electric mixer on medium speed until they become frothy.
    - Add the cream of tartar and continue to beat the egg whites until soft peaks form.
3. Gradually Add Sugar:
    - While still beating, gradually add the granulated sugar to the egg whites, a spoonful at a time, until all the sugar has been incorporated.
    - Continue beating until the egg whites are glossy and stiff peaks form. Be careful not to overbeat.
4. Fold in Egg Yolks:
    - In a separate bowl, lightly beat the egg yolks.
    - Gently fold the beaten egg yolks into the whipped egg whites using a spatula, just until combined.
5. Pipe or Spoon the Mixture:
    - Transfer the egg mixture to a piping bag fitted with a large round tip, or simply use a spoon to drop dollops of the mixture onto the prepared baking sheet, leaving some space between each one.
6. Bake:
    - Place the baking sheet in the preheated oven and bake the Suspiros de Monja for about 15-20 minutes, or until they are lightly golden on the outside and set.
    - The pastries should be crisp on the outside but still soft and airy on the inside.

7. Cool and Dust:
    - Remove the Suspiros de Monja from the oven and let them cool on the baking sheet for a few minutes.
    - Transfer the pastries to a wire rack to cool completely.
    - Once cooled, dust the Suspiros de Monja with powdered sugar before serving.

These delicate pastries are best enjoyed fresh on the day they are made, but they can be stored in an airtight container at room temperature for a day or two. Serve them as a sweet treat alongside coffee or tea, or enjoy them on their own as a light and airy dessert.

**Gachas Manchegas (Manchego Porridge)**

Ingredients:

- 1 cup (125g) all-purpose flour
- 4 cups (960ml) water or milk (or a combination of both)
- Pinch of salt
- Sugar or honey, to taste (optional)
- Ground cinnamon, for garnish (optional)
- Lemon zest, for garnish (optional)

Instructions:

1. Mix Flour with Water/Milk:
    - In a saucepan, whisk together the flour and water or milk until well combined. If you prefer a thicker consistency, use less liquid.
2. Cook the Mixture:
    - Place the saucepan over medium heat and bring the mixture to a simmer, stirring constantly to prevent lumps from forming.
    - Once the mixture starts to simmer, reduce the heat to low and continue to cook, stirring frequently, until the porridge thickens to your desired consistency. This usually takes about 10-15 minutes.
3. Season:
    - Add a pinch of salt to enhance the flavors of the porridge. You can also add sugar or honey to sweeten the porridge, if desired. Adjust the sweetness to your taste preferences.
4. Serve:
    - Once the porridge has reached your desired consistency and flavor, remove it from the heat.
    - Serve the Gachas Manchegas warm in individual bowls.
    - Optionally, garnish each serving with a sprinkle of ground cinnamon and/or lemon zest for added flavor and presentation.

Gachas Manchegas can be enjoyed as a comforting breakfast dish or as a simple dessert. It's versatile enough to be customized with various toppings or flavorings according to your taste. Some people like to enjoy it with a drizzle of olive oil or with savory additions like crumbled cheese or diced ham. Experiment with different variations to find your favorite way to enjoy this traditional Spanish porridge!

**Buñuelos de Viento (Spanish Wind Fritters)**

Ingredients:

- 1 cup (240ml) water
- 1/2 cup (115g) unsalted butter
- 1 cup (125g) all-purpose flour
- Pinch of salt
- 4 large eggs
- Zest of 1 lemon or orange
- Vegetable oil, for frying
- Powdered sugar, for dusting

Instructions:

1. Prepare the Dough:
    - In a saucepan, combine the water and butter over medium heat. Bring to a boil, then reduce the heat to low.
    - Add the flour and a pinch of salt to the saucepan all at once, stirring quickly with a wooden spoon until the mixture forms a smooth dough and pulls away from the sides of the pan. This should take about 1-2 minutes.
2. Cool the Dough:
    - Transfer the dough to a mixing bowl and let it cool slightly, about 5 minutes.
3. Add Eggs and Citrus Zest:
    - Add the eggs, one at a time, to the slightly cooled dough, beating well after each addition until the eggs are fully incorporated.
    - Stir in the lemon or orange zest to add a subtle citrus flavor to the dough.
4. Fry the Buñuelos:
    - In a deep frying pan or pot, heat vegetable oil to 350°F (180°C).
    - Drop spoonfuls of the dough into the hot oil, using a spoon or a small ice cream scoop. Fry the buñuelos in batches, being careful not to overcrowd the pan.
    - Fry the buñuelos for 2-3 minutes on each side, or until they are golden brown and puffed up.
    - Use a slotted spoon to transfer the fried buñuelos to a plate lined with paper towels to drain any excess oil.
5. Serve:

- Once the buñuelos are cool enough to handle but still warm, dust them generously with powdered sugar.
- Serve the Buñuelos de Viento warm as a delightful snack or dessert.

Buñuelos de Viento are best enjoyed fresh, but they can be stored in an airtight container at room temperature for a day or two. Reheat them briefly in the oven before serving to restore their crispiness. These light and fluffy fritters are sure to be a hit with family and friends!

**Brazo de Gitano (Spanish Swiss Roll)**

Sponge Cake Ingredients:

- 4 large eggs, at room temperature
- 1/2 cup (100g) granulated sugar
- 1 teaspoon vanilla extract
- 1/2 cup (60g) all-purpose flour
- 1/4 cup (30g) cornstarch
- 1 teaspoon baking powder
- Pinch of salt

Filling Ingredients:

- 1 cup (240ml) heavy cream, chilled
- 2 tablespoons powdered sugar (adjust to taste)
- 1 teaspoon vanilla extract
- 3/4 cup (180ml) fruit jam or spread of your choice (such as strawberry, raspberry, or apricot)

Instructions:

1. Preheat the Oven:
    - Preheat your oven to 350°F (175°C). Grease a 13x9-inch (33x23cm) baking pan and line it with parchment paper, leaving an overhang on the sides for easy removal.
2. Prepare the Sponge Cake:
    - In a mixing bowl, beat the eggs and granulated sugar together with an electric mixer on high speed until thick and pale in color, about 5 minutes.
    - Beat in the vanilla extract.
3. Sift Dry Ingredients:
    - In a separate bowl, sift together the all-purpose flour, cornstarch, baking powder, and salt.
4. Fold Dry Ingredients:
    - Gradually fold the sifted dry ingredients into the egg mixture, using a spatula, until just combined. Be gentle to maintain the airiness of the batter.
5. Bake the Cake:

- Pour the batter into the prepared baking pan and spread it evenly with a spatula.
- Bake in the preheated oven for 12-15 minutes, or until the cake is lightly golden and springs back when lightly pressed with your fingertip.

6. Roll the Cake:
   - While the cake is still warm, place a clean kitchen towel on a flat surface and dust it lightly with powdered sugar.
   - Carefully invert the baked cake onto the prepared towel. Peel off the parchment paper from the bottom of the cake.
   - Starting from one of the short ends, gently roll the cake and the towel together into a tight spiral. Allow the rolled cake to cool completely on a wire rack.
7. Prepare the Filling:
   - In a chilled mixing bowl, whip the heavy cream, powdered sugar, and vanilla extract together until stiff peaks form.
8. Fill and Roll:
   - Carefully unroll the cooled cake from the towel.
   - Spread an even layer of fruit jam or spread over the surface of the cake, leaving a small border around the edges.
   - Spread the whipped cream filling evenly over the jam layer.
9. Roll Again:
   - Starting from the same short end as before, gently roll the cake back up into a tight spiral, this time without the towel.
   - Place the rolled cake seam-side down on a serving platter.
10. Chill and Serve:
    - Wrap the Brazo de Gitano in plastic wrap and refrigerate for at least 1 hour before serving to allow the filling to set.
    - Before serving, dust the top of the cake with powdered sugar for a decorative finish.
    - Use a sharp knife to slice the Brazo de Gitano into individual servings, and enjoy!

Brazo de Gitano makes a stunning and delicious dessert for any occasion. Feel free to customize the filling with your favorite flavors or add a drizzle of chocolate ganache for extra indulgence!

**Yemas de Santa Teresa (Saint Teresa's Yolks)**

Ingredients:

- 12 large egg yolks
- 1 cup (200g) granulated sugar
- 1/2 cup (120ml) water
- Pinch of ground cinnamon (optional)
- Pinch of ground cloves (optional)
- Granulated sugar, for dusting (optional)

Instructions:

1. Prepare Egg Yolks:
    - Carefully separate the egg yolks from the egg whites, ensuring that there are no traces of egg whites in the yolks. You can use an egg separator or your hands to do this.
2. Make Sugar Syrup:
    - In a saucepan, combine the granulated sugar and water over medium heat, stirring until the sugar dissolves completely.
    - Bring the mixture to a gentle boil, then reduce the heat to low and simmer for about 5 minutes to create a sugar syrup. If using, add a pinch of ground cinnamon and ground cloves to the syrup for flavor.
3. Thicken Egg Yolks:
    - In a separate heatproof bowl, lightly beat the egg yolks.
    - Gradually pour the hot sugar syrup into the beaten egg yolks, whisking constantly to prevent the yolks from curdling.
4. Cook Mixture:
    - Transfer the egg yolk mixture back to the saucepan and place it over low heat.
    - Cook the mixture gently, stirring constantly with a wooden spoon, until it thickens and reaches a custard-like consistency. This usually takes about 10-15 minutes. Be patient and avoid overheating to prevent the yolks from curdling.
5. Shape Yemas:
    - Once the mixture has thickened, remove it from the heat and let it cool slightly.

- Using a spoon or your hands, shape the mixture into small balls or oval-shaped candies. You can also use candy molds for more uniform shapes.
6. Optional Dusting:
   - If desired, roll the shaped yemas in granulated sugar to coat them lightly.
7. Serve and Store:
   - Allow the Yemas de Santa Teresa to cool completely before serving.
   - Serve the candies on a platter or in decorative candy cups.
   - Store any leftover Yemas de Santa Teresa in an airtight container in the refrigerator for up to a week.

Yemas de Santa Teresa are a delightful treat that can be enjoyed on their own or as part of a dessert platter. They are often served during special occasions, religious festivities, or as gifts to friends and family. Their rich flavor and smooth texture make them a beloved delicacy in Spanish cuisine.

**Pestinos de Miel (Honey Cakes)**

Ingredients:

- 4 cups (500g) all-purpose flour
- 1 teaspoon ground cinnamon
- 1/4 teaspoon ground anise seeds (optional)
- Pinch of salt
- 1/2 cup (120ml) dry white wine
- 1/2 cup (120ml) extra virgin olive oil
- Vegetable oil, for frying
- Honey, for drizzling

Instructions:

1. Prepare the Dough:
    - In a large mixing bowl, combine the flour, cinnamon, ground anise seeds (if using), and a pinch of salt.
    - Make a well in the center of the dry ingredients and pour in the dry white wine and olive oil.
    - Mix until a dough forms, then knead the dough until smooth. Cover with a kitchen towel and let it rest for about 30 minutes.
2. Shape and Fry:
    - Roll out the dough on a lightly floured surface to about 1/8 inch (3mm) thickness.
    - Cut the dough into small rectangles or diamond shapes.
    - Heat vegetable oil in a deep frying pan to 350°F (180°C).
    - Fry the dough pieces in batches until golden brown, about 2-3 minutes per side.
    - Remove from the oil and drain on paper towels.
3. Drizzle with Honey:
    - While still warm, drizzle the pestinos generously with honey.
4. Serve:
    - Allow the pestinos to cool slightly before serving. Enjoy as a sweet treat with a cup of coffee or tea.

**Bollos de Aceite (Olive Oil Buns):**

Ingredients:

- 3 cups (375g) all-purpose flour
- 1/2 cup (120ml) extra virgin olive oil
- 1/2 cup (120ml) dry white wine
- 1/2 cup (100g) granulated sugar
- Zest of 1 lemon
- Zest of 1 orange
- 1 teaspoon baking powder
- Pinch of salt
- Sesame seeds, for sprinkling (optional)

Instructions:

1. Mix the Ingredients:
    - In a large mixing bowl, combine the flour, granulated sugar, lemon zest, orange zest, baking powder, and a pinch of salt.
    - Make a well in the center and pour in the olive oil and dry white wine.
    - Mix until a dough forms.
2. Knead and Rest:
    - Turn the dough out onto a lightly floured surface and knead it until smooth.
    - Cover the dough with a kitchen towel and let it rest for about 30 minutes.
3. Shape and Bake:
    - Preheat your oven to 350°F (175°C).
    - Divide the dough into small portions and shape each portion into a bun or ball.
    - Place the buns on a baking sheet lined with parchment paper.
    - Optional: Brush the tops of the buns with a little olive oil and sprinkle with sesame seeds.
    - Bake for about 15-20 minutes, or until the buns are golden brown and cooked through.
4. Serve:
    - Allow the Bollos de Aceite to cool slightly before serving.
    - Enjoy these delicious olive oil buns as a snack or accompaniment to your favorite dishes.

Both Pestinos de Miel and Bollos de Aceite are delightful Spanish treats that are perfect for enjoying with friends and family, especially during festive occasions or as a special treat.

**Tarta de Queso (Spanish Cheesecake)**

Ingredients:

- 1 1/2 pounds (680g) cream cheese, at room temperature
- 1 cup (200g) granulated sugar
- 4 large eggs, at room temperature
- 1/2 cup (120ml) heavy cream
- 1 teaspoon vanilla extract
- Zest of 1 lemon
- 2 tablespoons all-purpose flour
- Butter and flour, for greasing the pan

Instructions:

1. Preheat the Oven:
    - Preheat your oven to 350°F (175°C). Grease a 9-inch (23cm) springform pan with butter and lightly dust it with flour.
2. Prepare the Cream Cheese Mixture:
    - In a large mixing bowl, beat the cream cheese and granulated sugar together with an electric mixer until smooth and creamy.
    - Add the eggs one at a time, mixing well after each addition.
    - Stir in the heavy cream, vanilla extract, lemon zest, and all-purpose flour until well combined. The batter should be smooth and creamy.
3. Pour into Pan:
    - Pour the cream cheese mixture into the prepared springform pan, spreading it evenly with a spatula.
4. Bake:
    - Place the pan in the preheated oven and bake the cheesecake for about 45-55 minutes, or until the edges are set and the center is slightly jiggly.
5. Cool:
    - Once baked, remove the cheesecake from the oven and let it cool completely in the pan on a wire rack.
    - As the cheesecake cools, it will firm up and set.
6. Chill:
    - Once cooled to room temperature, transfer the cheesecake to the refrigerator and chill it for at least 4 hours, or preferably overnight. Chilling ensures that the cheesecake is firm and easy to slice.
7. Serve:

- Before serving, run a knife around the edge of the cheesecake to loosen it from the sides of the pan.
- Carefully remove the sides of the springform pan.
- Slice the Tarta de Queso into wedges and serve chilled.

Tarta de Queso is delicious on its own, but you can also serve it with fresh berries, fruit compote, or a drizzle of caramel sauce for added flavor and decoration. Enjoy this creamy and decadent Spanish cheesecake as a delightful dessert for any occasion!

**Goxua (Basque Dessert)**

Ingredients:

For the Sponge Cake:

- 4 large eggs, at room temperature
- 1/2 cup (100g) granulated sugar
- 1 teaspoon vanilla extract
- 1 cup (125g) all-purpose flour
- Pinch of salt

For the Pastry Cream (Crema Pastelera):

- 2 cups (480ml) whole milk
- 4 large egg yolks
- 1/2 cup (100g) granulated sugar
- 1/4 cup (30g) cornstarch
- 1 teaspoon vanilla extract

For Assembly:

- Whipped cream
- Granulated sugar, for caramelizing

Instructions:

1. Prepare the Sponge Cake:

    1. Preheat your oven to 350°F (175°C). Grease and flour a 9-inch (23cm) round cake pan.
    2. In a mixing bowl, beat the eggs and granulated sugar together with an electric mixer until pale and fluffy.
    3. Beat in the vanilla extract.
    4. Sift the flour and salt over the egg mixture and gently fold until just combined.
    5. Pour the batter into the prepared cake pan and spread it evenly.
    6. Bake for 20-25 minutes, or until the cake is golden brown and springs back when lightly pressed.
    7. Remove the cake from the oven and let it cool completely on a wire rack.

2. Prepare the Pastry Cream:

   1. In a saucepan, heat the milk over medium heat until it just begins to simmer. Remove from heat and set aside.
   2. In a separate bowl, whisk together the egg yolks, granulated sugar, and cornstarch until smooth and pale.
   3. Gradually pour the warm milk into the egg mixture, whisking constantly to prevent curdling.
   4. Return the mixture to the saucepan and place it over medium heat.
   5. Cook, stirring constantly, until the pastry cream thickens and coats the back of a spoon.
   6. Remove from heat and stir in the vanilla extract.
   7. Transfer the pastry cream to a bowl and cover it with plastic wrap, pressing the wrap directly onto the surface of the cream to prevent a skin from forming.
   8. Let the pastry cream cool to room temperature, then refrigerate it until chilled and firm.

3. Assembly:

   1. Once the sponge cake and pastry cream are cooled, assemble the Goxua.
   2. Cut the sponge cake into two layers horizontally.
   3. Place one layer of the sponge cake on a serving plate or cake stand.
   4. Spread a generous layer of pastry cream over the cake layer.
   5. Top the pastry cream with the second layer of sponge cake.
   6. Cover the top of the cake with whipped cream.
   7. Sprinkle granulated sugar evenly over the whipped cream layer.
   8. Use a kitchen torch to caramelize the sugar until it forms a golden-brown crust.
   9. Serve the Goxua chilled and enjoy its delicious layers of flavor and texture!

Goxua is a delightful dessert that combines the richness of pastry cream with the lightness of sponge cake and whipped cream, all topped with a caramelized sugar layer. It's perfect for special occasions or as a sweet treat to enjoy with friends and family.

**Croquetas de Chocolate (Chocolate Croquettes)**

Ingredients:

- 200g dark chocolate (at least 70% cocoa), chopped
- 1/2 cup (120ml) heavy cream
- 2 tablespoons unsalted butter
- 1/4 cup (50g) granulated sugar
- 1 teaspoon vanilla extract
- Pinch of salt
- 1 cup (100g) bread crumbs
- Vegetable oil, for frying
- Powdered sugar, for dusting (optional)
- Cocoa powder, for dusting (optional)

Instructions:

1. Prepare the Chocolate Ganache:
    - In a heatproof bowl, combine the chopped dark chocolate, heavy cream, unsalted butter, granulated sugar, vanilla extract, and a pinch of salt.
    - Place the bowl over a pot of simmering water (double boiler) and stir until the chocolate is completely melted and the mixture is smooth and glossy.
    - Remove the bowl from the heat and let the chocolate ganache cool to room temperature.
2. Shape the Croquettes:
    - Once the chocolate ganache has cooled and thickened slightly, use a spoon or a cookie scoop to portion out small balls of ganache.
    - Roll each portion into a ball between your palms, then roll them in the bread crumbs until evenly coated.
    - Place the coated chocolate balls on a baking sheet lined with parchment paper.
3. Chill the Croquettes:
    - Place the baking sheet with the coated chocolate balls in the refrigerator and chill for at least 30 minutes, or until firm.
4. Fry the Croquettes:
    - In a deep frying pan or pot, heat vegetable oil to 350°F (180°C).
    - Carefully drop the chilled chocolate croquettes into the hot oil, in batches, and fry until golden brown and crispy, about 1-2 minutes per batch.

- Use a slotted spoon to remove the fried croquettes from the oil and transfer them to a plate lined with paper towels to drain any excess oil.
5. Serve:
    - Once the chocolate croquettes have drained and cooled slightly, you can dust them with powdered sugar or cocoa powder for an extra touch of sweetness and presentation.
    - Serve the chocolate croquettes warm and enjoy their crispy exterior and gooey chocolate filling!

These chocolate croquettes are best enjoyed fresh and warm, but they can also be stored in an airtight container in the refrigerator for a day or two. Reheat them briefly in the oven before serving to restore their crispiness. They make a decadent dessert or sweet snack for any occasion!

**Frutas de Aragón (Aragonese Fruits)**

Ingredients:

- Whole cherries or apricots, pitted (fresh or preserved in syrup)
- Dark chocolate, chopped (or chocolate coating)
- Powdered sugar, for dusting (optional)

Instructions:

1. Prepare the Fruit:
    - If using fresh cherries or apricots, wash them thoroughly and remove the pits. If using preserved fruit, drain them well.
2. Dry the Fruit:
    - Pat the fruit dry with paper towels to remove any excess moisture. This will help the chocolate adhere better to the fruit.
3. Melt the Chocolate:
    - Place the chopped dark chocolate in a heatproof bowl.
    - Melt the chocolate using a double boiler or in the microwave in short bursts, stirring frequently until smooth and completely melted.
4. Coat the Fruit:
    - Using a fork or a toothpick, dip each cherry or apricot into the melted chocolate, making sure it is completely coated.
    - Allow any excess chocolate to drip off, then place the chocolate-coated fruit on a baking sheet lined with parchment paper.
5. Set the Chocolate:
    - Place the baking sheet with the chocolate-coated fruit in the refrigerator for about 15-20 minutes, or until the chocolate has hardened.
6. Dust with Powdered Sugar (Optional):
    - Once the chocolate has set, you can optionally dust the Frutas de Aragón with powdered sugar for an extra touch of sweetness and decoration.
7. Serve and Enjoy:
    - Once the chocolate has hardened and any powdered sugar has been added, the Frutas de Aragón are ready to be enjoyed!
    - Serve them as a sweet snack or dessert, or package them up in pretty boxes to give as gifts.

Frutas de Aragón are a delightful treat that combines the natural sweetness of fruit with the rich indulgence of chocolate. They are perfect for special occasions, holidays, or any time you're craving something sweet and delicious!

**Magdalenas (Spanish Muffins)**

Ingredients:

- 3 large eggs, at room temperature
- 1 cup (200g) granulated sugar
- 1 cup (240ml) vegetable oil or melted butter
- 1/2 cup (120ml) milk
- Zest of 1 lemon
- Zest of 1 orange
- 2 cups (250g) all-purpose flour
- 2 teaspoons baking powder
- Pinch of salt
- Granulated sugar, for sprinkling (optional)

Instructions:

1. Preheat the Oven:
    - Preheat your oven to 375°F (190°C). Line a muffin tin with paper liners or grease the cups with butter or cooking spray.
2. Prepare the Batter:
    - In a large mixing bowl, beat the eggs and granulated sugar together with an electric mixer until pale and fluffy.
    - Gradually add the vegetable oil or melted butter while continuing to beat the mixture.
    - Mix in the milk and the zest of the lemon and orange until well combined.
3. Combine Dry Ingredients:
    - In a separate bowl, sift together the all-purpose flour, baking powder, and a pinch of salt.
4. Mix Wet and Dry Ingredients:
    - Gradually add the dry ingredients to the wet ingredients, mixing until just combined. Be careful not to overmix, as this can result in tough muffins.
5. Fill Muffin Cups:
    - Spoon the batter into the prepared muffin cups, filling each about 2/3 full.
6. Bake:
    - Place the muffin tin in the preheated oven and bake the Magdalenas for 15-20 minutes, or until they are golden brown and a toothpick inserted into the center comes out clean.
7. Cool and Serve:

- Remove the Magdalenas from the oven and let them cool in the muffin tin for a few minutes before transferring them to a wire rack to cool completely.
- Once cooled, you can optionally sprinkle the tops of the Magdalenas with granulated sugar for added sweetness and texture.

8. Enjoy:
    - Serve the Magdalenas as a delicious breakfast or snack, either warm or at room temperature.
    - They pair wonderfully with a cup of coffee or tea, or enjoy them on their own for a delightful treat!

Magdalenas are best enjoyed fresh on the day they are made, but they can be stored in an airtight container at room temperature for a couple of days. They also freeze well, so you can make a batch ahead of time and thaw them as needed for a quick and convenient snack.

**Tejas (Spanish Lace Cookies)**

Ingredients:

- 1/2 cup (115g) unsalted butter
- 1/2 cup (100g) granulated sugar
- 1/4 cup (60ml) heavy cream
- 1/4 cup (30g) all-purpose flour
- 1/4 cup (30g) almond meal (ground almonds)
- 1 teaspoon vanilla extract
- Pinch of salt
- Sliced almonds (optional, for garnish)
- Melted chocolate (optional, for drizzling)

Instructions:

1. Preheat the Oven:
    - Preheat your oven to 350°F (175°C). Line a baking sheet with parchment paper or a silicone baking mat.
2. Prepare the Batter:
    - In a saucepan, melt the unsalted butter over medium heat.
    - Add the granulated sugar and heavy cream to the melted butter, stirring until the sugar is dissolved.
    - Remove the saucepan from the heat and let the mixture cool slightly.
3. Add Dry Ingredients:
    - Stir in the all-purpose flour, almond meal, vanilla extract, and a pinch of salt into the butter-sugar mixture until smooth.
4. Form the Cookies:
    - Drop teaspoonfuls of the batter onto the prepared baking sheet, spacing them a few inches apart as they will spread during baking.
    - Optionally, place a few sliced almonds on top of each cookie for garnish.
5. Bake:
    - Bake the cookies in the preheated oven for 8-10 minutes, or until they are golden brown around the edges.
    - Keep an eye on them as they bake, as they can quickly go from golden brown to burnt.
6. Shape the Cookies:
    - As soon as the cookies come out of the oven, use a spatula or the back of a spoon to gently shape them while they are still warm and pliable.

- You can shape them into cylinders or cones by rolling them around the handle of a wooden spoon or a similar utensil. Be careful as they will be hot.

7. Cool:
   - Transfer the shaped cookies to a wire rack to cool completely. They will firm up and become crispy as they cool.
8. Optional Drizzle:
   - Once the cookies have cooled, you can optionally drizzle them with melted chocolate for added flavor and decoration. Let the chocolate set before serving.
9. Serve and Enjoy:
   - Serve the Tejas as a delicate and crispy treat with a cup of coffee or tea, or enjoy them on their own as a sweet indulgence!

Tejas are best stored in an airtight container at room temperature. They can be enjoyed for several days, although they may lose some of their crispiness over time.

**Cocas de San Juan (Saint John's Cakes)**

Ingredients:

For the Dough:

- 4 cups (500g) all-purpose flour
- 1/2 cup (100g) granulated sugar
- 1/2 cup (120ml) olive oil or vegetable oil
- 1/2 cup (120ml) warm water
- 1 packet (7g) active dry yeast
- Pinch of salt

For the Topping (Optional, can vary):

- Sliced fruits (such as peaches, apricots, or figs)
- Nuts (such as almonds or walnuts)
- Granulated sugar
- Honey

Instructions:

1. Activate the Yeast:
    - In a small bowl, dissolve the yeast in warm water according to the package instructions. Let it sit for about 5-10 minutes, or until foamy.
2. Prepare the Dough:
    - In a large mixing bowl, combine the flour, granulated sugar, and a pinch of salt.
    - Make a well in the center of the dry ingredients and pour in the activated yeast mixture and olive oil.
    - Mix the ingredients together until a dough forms. If the dough is too dry, you can add a little more warm water, 1 tablespoon at a time, until it comes together.
    - Knead the dough on a lightly floured surface for about 5-7 minutes, or until it becomes smooth and elastic.
3. Let the Dough Rise:
    - Place the dough in a lightly oiled bowl, cover it with a clean kitchen towel or plastic wrap, and let it rise in a warm, draft-free place for about 1-2 hours, or until it doubles in size.

4. Preheat the Oven:
    - Preheat your oven to 375°F (190°C). Line a baking sheet with parchment paper.
5. Shape the Cocas:
    - Once the dough has risen, punch it down to deflate it, then divide it into equal portions, depending on how many Cocas you want to make.
    - Roll out each portion of dough into a flat round or oval shape, about 1/4 inch (6mm) thick, and place it on the prepared baking sheet.
6. Add Toppings (Optional):
    - Arrange sliced fruits or nuts on top of the dough, pressing them gently into the surface.
    - Sprinkle the Cocas with granulated sugar for added sweetness.
7. Bake:
    - Bake the Cocas in the preheated oven for 15-20 minutes, or until they are golden brown and cooked through.
8. Serve:
    - Once baked, remove the Cocas from the oven and let them cool slightly on the baking sheet.
    - Drizzle with honey before serving if desired.

Cocas de San Juan are best enjoyed fresh on the day they are made, but they can be stored in an airtight container at room temperature for a day or two. They are a delicious way to celebrate Saint John's Eve and are often enjoyed with family and friends during this festive occasion.

**Mostachones de Utrera (Utrera Mustachios)**

Ingredients:

- 2 cups (250g) almond flour or finely ground almonds
- 1 cup (200g) granulated sugar
- Zest of 1 lemon
- 2 large eggs
- 1/4 cup (60ml) olive oil or melted butter
- 1/4 teaspoon ground cinnamon
- Pinch of salt
- Powdered sugar, for dusting (optional)

Instructions:

1. Preheat the Oven:
    - Preheat your oven to 350°F (175°C). Line a baking sheet with parchment paper.
2. Mix Dry Ingredients:
    - In a large mixing bowl, combine the almond flour, granulated sugar, lemon zest, ground cinnamon, and a pinch of salt. Stir until well mixed.
3. Add Wet Ingredients:
    - Add the eggs and olive oil (or melted butter) to the dry ingredients. Mix until a thick dough forms. If the dough is too dry, you can add a little more olive oil or melted butter.
4. Shape the Cookies:
    - Take small portions of the dough and roll them into balls, about 1 inch (2.5cm) in diameter.
    - Place the balls of dough onto the prepared baking sheet, spacing them a few inches apart. Flatten each ball slightly with the palm of your hand.
5. Bake:
    - Bake the cookies in the preheated oven for 12-15 minutes, or until they are golden brown around the edges.
6. Cool:
    - Once baked, remove the cookies from the oven and let them cool on the baking sheet for a few minutes before transferring them to a wire rack to cool completely.
7. Dust with Powdered Sugar (Optional):

- Once the cookies have cooled, you can dust them with powdered sugar for a decorative finish. Simply sift powdered sugar over the top of the cookies using a fine-mesh sieve.
8. Serve and Enjoy:
    - Mostachones de Utrera are best enjoyed at room temperature. Serve them as a sweet treat with a cup of coffee or tea, or enjoy them as a dessert after a meal.

These Mostachones de Utrera are a delicious and traditional Spanish delicacy, perfect for sharing with family and friends or for enjoying on your own as a special treat. Their rich almond flavor and delicate texture make them a delightful addition to any occasion.

**Piononos (Andalusian Dessert)**

Ingredients:

For the Sponge Cake:

- 6 large eggs
- 3/4 cup (150g) granulated sugar
- 3/4 cup (90g) all-purpose flour
- 1 teaspoon vanilla extract

For the Filling:

- 2 cups (480ml) whole milk
- 4 large egg yolks
- 1/2 cup (100g) granulated sugar
- 1/4 cup (30g) cornstarch
- 1 teaspoon vanilla extract
- 1/4 cup (60ml) rum or other liqueur (optional)
- Zest of 1 lemon (optional)

For Assembling and Topping:

- Powdered sugar, for dusting

Instructions:

1. Make the Sponge Cake:

    1. Preheat your oven to 350°F (175°C). Grease and line a jelly roll pan (approximately 10x15 inches) with parchment paper.
    2. In a large mixing bowl, beat the eggs and granulated sugar together with an electric mixer until pale and fluffy, about 5-7 minutes.
    3. Gently fold in the flour and vanilla extract until just combined.
    4. Pour the batter into the prepared pan and spread it out evenly.
    5. Bake for 10-12 minutes, or until the cake is lightly golden and springs back when touched.
    6. Remove the cake from the oven and let it cool in the pan for a few minutes. Then, transfer it to a wire rack to cool completely.

2. Make the Filling:

   1. In a saucepan, heat the milk over medium heat until it just begins to simmer. Remove from heat and set aside.
   2. In a separate bowl, whisk together the egg yolks, granulated sugar, and cornstarch until smooth and pale.
   3. Gradually pour the warm milk into the egg mixture, whisking constantly to prevent curdling.
   4. Return the mixture to the saucepan and place it over medium heat.
   5. Cook, stirring constantly, until the custard thickens and coats the back of a spoon.
   6. Remove from heat and stir in the vanilla extract and rum or other liqueur (if using). Add the lemon zest if desired.
   7. Transfer the custard to a bowl and let it cool to room temperature.

3. Assemble the Piononos:

   1. Once the sponge cake has cooled, spread the custard filling evenly over the surface of the cake.
   2. Starting from one of the short ends, carefully roll up the cake into a tight cylinder.
   3. Place the rolled cake seam-side down on a serving platter.

4. Serve and Enjoy:

   1. Trim the ends of the cake roll if desired for a neater presentation.
   2. Dust the top of the Pionono generously with powdered sugar.
   3. Slice the Pionono into rounds and serve.
   4. Enjoy the delicious Andalusian treat!

Piononos are best enjoyed fresh, but they can be stored in the refrigerator for a day or two. Remember to bring them to room temperature before serving for the best flavor and texture.

**Olla Podrida (Spanish Potpourri)**

Ingredients:

For the Stew:

- Assorted meats, such as beef, pork, chicken, chorizo, and/or ham, cut into chunks
- Assorted vegetables, such as onions, carrots, celery, potatoes, tomatoes, and/or bell peppers, chopped
- Assorted legumes, such as beans (white beans, kidney beans, chickpeas), lentils, and/or peas
- Garlic cloves, minced
- Bay leaves
- Paprika, cumin, and other spices, to taste
- Salt and pepper, to taste
- Olive oil
- Beef or chicken broth, or water

Instructions:

1. Prepare the Meats and Vegetables:
    - Season the meat chunks with salt, pepper, and any desired spices. Brown them in a large pot with a little olive oil over medium-high heat until golden brown on all sides. Remove and set aside.
    - In the same pot, sauté the chopped onions, carrots, celery, and any other desired vegetables until they start to soften.
2. Simmer the Stew:
    - Return the browned meat to the pot. Add minced garlic, bay leaves, paprika, cumin, and any other desired spices.
    - Add the assorted legumes and cover everything with beef or chicken broth, or water.
    - Bring the stew to a boil, then reduce the heat to low and let it simmer gently, partially covered, for 1.5 to 2 hours, or until the meats and legumes are tender and the flavors have melded together. Stir occasionally and add more liquid if needed.
3. Adjust Seasoning and Serve:
    - Taste the stew and adjust the seasoning with salt, pepper, and spices as needed.

- Once the stew is ready, remove the bay leaves and serve it hot in deep bowls.
4. Optional Garnishes:
    - Garnish each serving of Olla Podrida with chopped fresh parsley or cilantro for a burst of freshness.
    - Serve with crusty bread or cooked rice on the side, if desired.

Olla Podrida is a comforting and satisfying dish that's perfect for cooler weather or for feeding a crowd. Its versatility allows for endless variations, making it a favorite in Spanish households and a beloved symbol of Spanish culinary tradition.

**Cuajada (Spanish Curd)**

Ingredients:

- 4 cups (1 liter) whole milk
- 1/4 cup (60ml) water
- 1/4 teaspoon calcium chloride (optional, helps with curdling)
- 1/4 teaspoon liquid rennet or 1/2 tablet rennet, dissolved in 1/4 cup (60ml) water
- Sugar or honey, to taste (optional)
- Ground cinnamon or fruit for topping (optional)

Instructions:

1. Prepare the Milk Mixture:
    - In a saucepan, heat the whole milk over medium heat until it reaches a temperature of around 95-100°C (200-212°F). Be careful not to let it boil.
2. Add Coagulating Agents:
    - If using calcium chloride, dissolve it in 1/4 cup of water and add it to the heated milk, stirring gently.
    - Next, add the dissolved rennet to the milk, stirring gently to distribute it evenly.
3. Allow the Mixture to Set:
    - Remove the saucepan from the heat and cover it with a clean kitchen towel or lid.
    - Let the milk mixture sit undisturbed at room temperature for about 1-2 hours, or until it has thickened into a curd-like consistency. The exact time may vary depending on factors such as the temperature of the room and the freshness of the rennet.
4. Cut and Strain the Curds:
    - Once the mixture has set, use a knife to cut the curds into small squares or cubes directly in the saucepan.
    - Carefully strain the curds and whey through a fine-mesh sieve or cheesecloth-lined colander, allowing the whey to drain away. You can save the whey for other culinary uses or discard it.
5. Sweeten and Flavor (Optional):
    - Transfer the strained curds to serving dishes and sweeten them to taste with sugar or honey, if desired.
    - Optionally, sprinkle ground cinnamon over the top or add slices of fruit for additional flavor and decoration.

6. Chill and Serve:
    - Refrigerate the Cuajada for at least 1-2 hours, or until it is chilled and set.
    - Serve the Cuajada cold as a refreshing and creamy dessert.

Cuajada can be enjoyed on its own as a simple dessert, or it can be served with toppings such as fruit, nuts, or a drizzle of honey for added flavor and texture. It's a versatile dessert that can be customized to suit your taste preferences, making it a favorite among those who appreciate traditional Spanish cuisine.

**Torrejas de Almendra (Almond Toast)**

Ingredients:

For the Almond Syrup:

- 1 cup (200g) granulated sugar
- 1 cup (240ml) water
- 1/2 cup (60g) almond meal or finely ground almonds
- 1 teaspoon almond extract (optional)
- 1 cinnamon stick (optional)

For the Torrejas:

- 6-8 slices of day-old bread, such as French bread or brioche
- 2-3 large eggs
- Butter or vegetable oil, for frying
- Powdered sugar, for dusting (optional)
- Sliced almonds, for garnish (optional)

Instructions:

1. Prepare the Almond Syrup:

   1. In a saucepan, combine the granulated sugar, water, almond meal (or ground almonds), almond extract (if using), and cinnamon stick (if using).
   2. Bring the mixture to a simmer over medium heat, stirring occasionally until the sugar is completely dissolved.
   3. Reduce the heat to low and let the syrup simmer gently for about 5-7 minutes, allowing the flavors to meld together.
   4. Remove the syrup from the heat and let it cool slightly. Strain the syrup through a fine-mesh sieve to remove any almond meal or cinnamon stick. Set the syrup aside to cool completely.

2. Prepare the Torrejas:

   1. In a shallow dish, beat the eggs until well mixed. Set aside.
   2. Cut the slices of bread into thick slices, about 1 inch (2.5 cm) thick.

3. Heat a skillet or frying pan over medium heat and add a tablespoon of butter or vegetable oil.
4. Dip each slice of bread into the beaten eggs, coating both sides evenly.
5. Place the coated bread slices in the hot skillet and cook until golden brown and crispy on both sides, about 2-3 minutes per side.
6. Remove the cooked Torrejas from the skillet and place them on a plate lined with paper towels to drain any excess oil.

3. Assemble and Serve:

1. Once all the Torrejas are cooked, place them in a shallow dish or baking dish.
2. Pour the cooled almond syrup over the Torrejas, making sure to coat each slice evenly.
3. Let the Torrejas soak in the syrup for a few minutes, allowing them to absorb the flavors.
4. Optionally, sprinkle powdered sugar over the Torrejas and garnish with sliced almonds before serving.
5. Serve the Torrejas de Almendra warm as a deliciously sweet and aromatic dessert.

Torrejas de Almendra are best enjoyed fresh and warm, but they can also be served at room temperature. They make a delightful treat for breakfast, brunch, or dessert, and their almond-infused flavor adds a special touch to any occasion.

**Pestiños de Cádiz (Cadiz Honey Cakes)**

Ingredients:

For the Dough:

- 4 cups (500g) all-purpose flour
- 1 teaspoon baking powder
- 1/4 teaspoon salt
- 1/2 cup (120ml) dry white wine (such as fino or manzanilla)
- 1/2 cup (120ml) olive oil or vegetable oil

For Frying:

- Vegetable oil, for frying

For the Honey Syrup:

- 1 cup (240ml) honey
- 1/2 cup (120ml) water
- 1 cinnamon stick
- 3 whole cloves
- 1 strip of lemon peel
- 1 strip of orange peel

For Dusting (Optional):

- Ground cinnamon
- Powdered sugar

Instructions:

1. Prepare the Dough:

   1. In a large mixing bowl, sift together the all-purpose flour, baking powder, and salt.
   2. Make a well in the center of the dry ingredients and pour in the dry white wine and olive oil.

3. Mix the ingredients together until a smooth dough forms. If the dough is too dry, you can add a little more wine or water, 1 tablespoon at a time, until it comes together.
4. Knead the dough on a lightly floured surface for a few minutes until it is smooth and elastic. Then, cover the dough with plastic wrap and let it rest at room temperature for about 30 minutes.

2. Shape and Fry the Pestiños:

1. After the dough has rested, divide it into smaller portions and roll each portion out thinly on a floured surface, to about 1/8 inch (3mm) thickness.
2. Use a knife or pastry cutter to cut the rolled-out dough into rectangles or diamond shapes, about 3-4 inches (7-10cm) long.
3. Heat vegetable oil in a deep frying pan or pot to 350°F (175°C).
4. Carefully add the shaped dough pieces to the hot oil, a few at a time, and fry them until golden brown and crispy, about 2-3 minutes per side.
5. Use a slotted spoon to transfer the fried Pestiños to a plate lined with paper towels to drain any excess oil.

3. Make the Honey Syrup:

1. In a saucepan, combine the honey, water, cinnamon stick, whole cloves, lemon peel, and orange peel.
2. Bring the mixture to a simmer over medium heat, stirring occasionally, until the honey is completely dissolved and the syrup has thickened slightly, about 5-7 minutes.
3. Remove the saucepan from the heat and let the syrup cool slightly. Then, strain it to remove the spices and citrus peels.

4. Soak and Serve:

1. While the syrup is still warm, dip the fried Pestiños into the syrup, coating them evenly.
2. Let the Pestiños soak in the syrup for a few minutes to absorb the flavors.
3. Optionally, dust the Pestiños with ground cinnamon or powdered sugar before serving.
4. Serve the Pestiños de Cádiz warm or at room temperature as a deliciously sweet and aromatic treat.

Pestiños de Cádiz are best enjoyed fresh on the day they are made, but they can also be stored in an airtight container at room temperature for a day or two. They are a delightful indulgence for any occasion and are sure to be a hit with family and friends!

**Torta de La Serena (La Serena Cheese Cake)**

Ingredients:

For the crust:

- 200g (about 7 oz) of digestive biscuits or graham crackers
- 100g (about 3.5 oz) of unsalted butter, melted

For the filling:

- 500g (about 18 oz) of Torta del Casar cheese (or similar soft sheep's milk cheese)
- 4 large eggs
- 150g (about 5.3 oz) of granulated sugar
- Zest of one lemon (optional)
- Pinch of cinnamon (optional)

Instructions:

1. Preheat your oven to 180°C (about 350°F).
2. Start by making the crust. Crush the digestive biscuits or graham crackers into fine crumbs. You can do this by placing them in a plastic bag and using a rolling pin, or by pulsing them in a food processor.
3. Mix the biscuit or cracker crumbs with the melted butter until well combined. Press the mixture firmly into the bottom of a springform pan (about 9 inches in diameter), creating an even layer. You can also press some of the mixture up the sides of the pan if you like.
4. In a large mixing bowl, beat the Torta del Casar cheese until smooth. You can use a hand mixer or a stand mixer for this.
5. Add the eggs, one at a time, to the cheese, beating well after each addition.
6. Gradually add the granulated sugar to the cheese mixture, continuing to beat until smooth and creamy. If using, mix in the lemon zest and cinnamon at this stage.
7. Pour the cheese mixture over the prepared crust in the springform pan, spreading it out evenly.

8. Bake the cheesecake in the preheated oven for about 40-45 minutes, or until the top is set and slightly golden.
9. Once baked, remove the cheesecake from the oven and let it cool completely at room temperature. Then, refrigerate it for at least a few hours or overnight until chilled and set.
10. When ready to serve, carefully remove the sides of the springform pan and transfer the cheesecake to a serving plate. Optionally, drizzle some honey over the top or serve with fruit preserves.

Enjoy your delicious Torta de La Serena!

**Arrop i tallaetes (Valencian Molasses and Dough)**

Ingredients:

For the arrop:

- 1 liter (about 4 cups) of grape juice (freshly squeezed if possible)
- Sugar (optional, depending on the sweetness of the grapes)

For the tallaetes:

- Loaf of bread, preferably a rustic country-style bread
- Olive oil (for brushing the bread)
- Sugar (for sprinkling on the bread, optional)

Instructions:

1. Start by making the arrop. In a large saucepan, bring the grape juice to a simmer over medium heat. If the grapes used for the juice aren't very sweet, you can add some sugar to taste.
2. Allow the grape juice to simmer gently, stirring occasionally, until it reduces by about half and becomes thick and syrupy. This can take anywhere from 1 to 2 hours, depending on the heat and the consistency you desire. Be careful not to let it burn.
3. While the arrop is simmering, prepare the tallaetes. Preheat your oven to 180°C (about 350°F).
4. Slice the loaf of bread into thin strips, about 1/4 to 1/2 inch thick. Place the bread strips on a baking sheet lined with parchment paper.
5. Lightly brush each bread strip with olive oil and sprinkle with sugar if desired.
6. Bake the bread strips in the preheated oven for about 10-15 minutes, or until they are golden brown and crisp. Keep an eye on them to prevent burning.
7. Once the arrop has reached your desired consistency, remove it from the heat and let it cool slightly.

8. To serve, drizzle the warm arrop over the crispy tallaetes. The combination of the sweet molasses with the crunchy bread strips creates a delicious contrast of flavors and textures.

Arrop i tallaetes is typically enjoyed as a dessert or snack, and it's perfect for dipping the bread strips into the molasses. It's a wonderful taste of traditional Valencian cuisine that's easy to make at home.

**Tarta de Manzana (Spanish Apple Tart)**

Ingredients:

For the pastry:

- 200g (about 1 1/2 cups) all-purpose flour
- 100g (about 1/2 cup) unsalted butter, cold and cubed
- 1 tablespoon granulated sugar
- Pinch of salt
- 1 large egg, beaten (for egg wash)

For the filling:

- 4-5 medium-sized apples (such as Granny Smith or Golden Delicious), peeled, cored, and thinly sliced
- 2 tablespoons granulated sugar
- 1 teaspoon ground cinnamon
- Zest of 1 lemon
- Juice of 1/2 lemon

For the glaze (optional):

- 2 tablespoons apricot jam or apple jelly
- 1 tablespoon water

Instructions:

1. Preheat your oven to 180°C (about 350°F). Grease a 9-inch tart pan with a removable bottom, or you can use a pie dish if you don't have a tart pan.
2. To make the pastry, in a large mixing bowl, combine the flour, sugar, and salt. Add the cold cubed butter and rub it into the flour mixture using your fingertips or a pastry cutter until the mixture resembles coarse breadcrumbs.

3. Add the beaten egg to the mixture and gently knead until the dough comes together. Be careful not to overwork the dough. Shape the dough into a disk, wrap it in plastic wrap, and refrigerate for at least 30 minutes.
4. In a separate bowl, toss the thinly sliced apples with the granulated sugar, ground cinnamon, lemon zest, and lemon juice until well coated. Set aside.
5. Once the dough has chilled, remove it from the refrigerator and roll it out on a lightly floured surface into a circle about 12 inches in diameter and 1/8 inch thick.
6. Carefully transfer the rolled-out pastry to the prepared tart pan, pressing it gently into the bottom and up the sides of the pan. Trim any excess pastry from the edges.
7. Arrange the sliced apples in concentric circles over the pastry, slightly overlapping them as you go.
8. Fold any overhanging pastry over the edge of the apples, or you can leave it rustic if you prefer.
9. Brush the edges of the pastry with the beaten egg wash.
10. Bake the tart in the preheated oven for 35-40 minutes, or until the pastry is golden brown and the apples are tender.
11. If using the glaze, in a small saucepan, heat the apricot jam or apple jelly with the water over low heat until melted and smooth. Brush the glaze over the warm tart.
12. Allow the tart to cool slightly before serving. You can serve it warm or at room temperature. Optionally, serve with a dollop of whipped cream or a scoop of vanilla ice cream.

Enjoy your delicious Spanish Apple Tart!

**Melindres (Spanish Sweet Breadsticks)**

Ingredients:

- 2 cups (250g) all-purpose flour
- 2 teaspoons baking powder
- 1/4 teaspoon salt
- 1/4 cup (50g) granulated sugar
- Zest of 1 lemon
- 1 teaspoon anise seeds
- 2 large eggs
- 1/4 cup (60ml) milk
- 1/4 cup (60ml) vegetable oil
- Granulated sugar, for coating

Instructions:

1. Preheat your oven to 180°C (about 350°F). Line a baking sheet with parchment paper or lightly grease it.
2. In a mixing bowl, sift together the flour, baking powder, and salt.
3. In another bowl, combine the granulated sugar, lemon zest, and anise seeds. Rub the mixture between your fingers to release the flavors of the lemon zest and anise seeds.
4. Add the eggs, milk, and vegetable oil to the sugar mixture. Whisk until well combined.
5. Gradually add the dry ingredients to the wet ingredients, stirring until a soft dough forms. You may need to use your hands to knead the dough gently until smooth.
6. Divide the dough into small portions and roll each portion into a long, thin rope, about 1/2 inch in diameter. Cut the ropes into pieces, each about 4 inches long.
7. Place the dough pieces on the prepared baking sheet, leaving some space between them.
8. Bake the melindres in the preheated oven for 12-15 minutes, or until they are lightly golden brown.
9. While the melindres are still warm, roll them in granulated sugar to coat them evenly.
10. Allow the melindres to cool completely on a wire rack before serving.

Enjoy your homemade melindres with a cup of coffee or tea for a delightful Spanish treat!

**Mantecadas de Astorga (Astorga Shortbread)**

Ingredients:

- 250g (about 2 cups) all-purpose flour
- 200g (about 1 cup) granulated sugar
- 200g (about 1 cup) unsalted butter, at room temperature
- 4 large eggs
- Zest of 1 lemon
- 1 teaspoon ground cinnamon
- 1/2 teaspoon baking powder
- Pinch of salt

Instructions:

1. Preheat your oven to 180°C (about 350°F). Grease a muffin tin or mantecadas molds with butter or non-stick cooking spray.
2. In a mixing bowl, sift together the flour, baking powder, ground cinnamon, and salt. Set aside.
3. In another bowl, cream together the butter and sugar until light and fluffy.
4. Add the eggs, one at a time, beating well after each addition.
5. Stir in the lemon zest until well combined.
6. Gradually add the dry ingredients to the wet ingredients, mixing until a smooth batter forms. Be careful not to overmix.
7. Spoon the batter into the prepared muffin tin or mantecadas molds, filling each cavity about 3/4 full.
8. Bake in the preheated oven for 15-20 minutes, or until the mantecadas are lightly golden brown and a toothpick inserted into the center comes out clean.
9. Remove the mantecadas from the oven and let them cool in the tin or molds for a few minutes before transferring them to a wire rack to cool completely.
10. Once cooled, dust the mantecadas with powdered sugar before serving.

These Astorga Shortbread cookies are perfect for enjoying with a cup of coffee or tea, or as a sweet treat any time of the day. They have a delicate crumb and a wonderful aroma from the lemon zest and cinnamon. Enjoy!

**Fardelejos (Aragonese Pastries)**

Ingredients:

For the pastry:

- 200g (about 1 3/4 cups) ground almonds
- 200g (about 1 cup) granulated sugar
- 3 large eggs
- Zest of 1 lemon
- 1/2 teaspoon ground cinnamon
- Pinch of salt

For the coating:

- Granulated sugar, for coating

Instructions:

1. Preheat your oven to 180°C (about 350°F). Line a baking sheet with parchment paper.
2. In a mixing bowl, combine the ground almonds, granulated sugar, lemon zest, ground cinnamon, and a pinch of salt.
3. Separate the egg yolks from the egg whites. Reserve the egg whites for later use.
4. Add the egg yolks to the almond mixture and mix until well combined. The mixture should come together to form a thick dough.
5. Divide the dough into small portions and shape each portion into an oval or rectangular shape, resembling a small log.
6. Place the shaped fardelejos onto the prepared baking sheet, leaving some space between each one.
7. In a small bowl, lightly beat the reserved egg whites. Brush the tops of the fardelejos with the beaten egg whites.
8. Sprinkle granulated sugar generously over the tops of the fardelejos, coating them evenly.

9. Bake in the preheated oven for 15-20 minutes, or until the fardelejos are lightly golden brown on the outside.
10. Remove the fardelejos from the oven and let them cool on the baking sheet for a few minutes before transferring them to a wire rack to cool completely.
11. Once cooled, the fardelejos are ready to be enjoyed! They can be served as a sweet snack or dessert, perfect with a cup of coffee or tea.

These traditional Aragonese pastries are simple to make and are sure to delight with their nutty flavor and sweet, chewy texture. Enjoy!

**Roscos de Anís (Aniseed Rings)**

Ingredients:

- 500g (about 4 cups) all-purpose flour
- 200g (about 1 cup) granulated sugar
- 100ml (about 7 tablespoons) olive oil
- 100ml (about 7 tablespoons) aniseed liqueur (such as Anís del Mono)
- Zest of 1 lemon
- 1 teaspoon ground aniseed (optional)
- 1 teaspoon baking powder
- Pinch of salt
- Additional granulated sugar, for coating

Instructions:

1. Preheat your oven to 180°C (about 350°F). Line a baking sheet with parchment paper or lightly grease it.
2. In a mixing bowl, sift together the flour, baking powder, and salt.
3. In another bowl, combine the granulated sugar, olive oil, aniseed liqueur, lemon zest, and ground aniseed (if using). Mix until well combined.
4. Gradually add the dry ingredients to the wet ingredients, mixing until a smooth dough forms. If the dough is too sticky, you can add a little more flour.
5. Take small portions of the dough and roll them into ropes about 1/2 inch in diameter. Shape each rope into a ring by joining the ends together.
6. Place the aniseed rings onto the prepared baking sheet, leaving some space between each one.
7. Bake in the preheated oven for 15-20 minutes, or until the roscos are lightly golden brown.
8. Remove the roscos from the oven and let them cool on the baking sheet for a few minutes.
9. While the roscos are still warm, roll them in granulated sugar to coat them evenly.
10. Allow the roscos to cool completely on a wire rack before serving.

These traditional Spanish Aniseed Rings are perfect for enjoying with a cup of coffee or tea, or as a sweet treat any time of the day. They have a delicate texture and a lovely aniseed flavor that is sure to delight your taste buds. Enjoy!

**Sobaos Pasiegos (Cantabrian Sponge Cakes)**

Ingredients:

- 250g (about 2 cups) all-purpose flour
- 250g (about 1 cup) granulated sugar
- 250g (about 1 cup) unsalted butter, at room temperature
- 4 large eggs
- Zest of 1 lemon
- 1/2 teaspoon ground cinnamon (optional)
- Pinch of salt

Instructions:

1. Preheat your oven to 180°C (about 350°F). Grease and flour a muffin tin or small cake molds. Alternatively, you can use paper liners.
2. In a mixing bowl, cream together the butter and sugar until light and fluffy.
3. Add the eggs, one at a time, beating well after each addition.
4. Stir in the lemon zest and ground cinnamon (if using).
5. Gradually add the flour and salt to the wet ingredients, mixing until well combined and a smooth batter forms.
6. Spoon the batter into the prepared muffin tin or cake molds, filling each cavity about 3/4 full.
7. Bake in the preheated oven for 20-25 minutes, or until the sobaos are golden brown on top and a toothpick inserted into the center comes out clean.
8. Remove the sobaos from the oven and let them cool in the tin or molds for a few minutes before transferring them to a wire rack to cool completely.
9. Once cooled, the sobaos pasiegos are ready to be enjoyed! They can be served warm or at room temperature.

These traditional Cantabrian sponge cakes are a delicious treat that showcases the flavors of the region. They have a wonderful buttery taste with a hint of citrus from the lemon zest, making them perfect for any occasion. Enjoy!

**Tarta de Queso y Membrillo (Cheese and Quince Tart)**

Ingredients:

For the crust:

- 200g (about 1 1/2 cups) digestive biscuits or graham crackers
- 100g (about 7 tablespoons) unsalted butter, melted

For the filling:

- 500g (about 2 cups) cream cheese, at room temperature
- 200g (about 1 cup) Greek yogurt
- 150g (about 3/4 cup) granulated sugar
- 3 large eggs
- 1 teaspoon vanilla extract
- Zest of 1 lemon
- 200g (about 7 oz) quince paste (membrillo), cut into small cubes

Instructions:

1. Preheat your oven to 180°C (about 350°F).
2. Start by making the crust. Crush the digestive biscuits or graham crackers into fine crumbs. You can do this by placing them in a plastic bag and using a rolling pin, or by pulsing them in a food processor.
3. Mix the biscuit or cracker crumbs with the melted butter until well combined. Press the mixture firmly into the bottom of a springform pan (about 9 inches in diameter), creating an even layer. You can also press some of the mixture up the sides of the pan if you like.
4. In a large mixing bowl, beat the cream cheese until smooth and creamy.
5. Add the Greek yogurt, granulated sugar, eggs, vanilla extract, and lemon zest to the cream cheese, and beat until well combined and smooth.
6. Pour the cream cheese mixture over the prepared crust in the springform pan, spreading it out evenly.

7. Scatter the cubes of quince paste evenly over the top of the cream cheese mixture.
8. Bake the tart in the preheated oven for about 40-45 minutes, or until the filling is set and slightly golden on top.
9. Once baked, remove the tart from the oven and let it cool completely at room temperature. Then, refrigerate it for at least a few hours or overnight until chilled and set.
10. When ready to serve, carefully remove the sides of the springform pan and transfer the tart to a serving plate.
11. Slice and serve the tart chilled, optionally with additional quince paste or a dollop of whipped cream on top.

Enjoy your delicious Cheese and Quince Tart!

**Gató Mallorquín (Mallorcan Almond Cake)**

Ingredients:

- 250g (about 2 1/2 cups) ground almonds
- 200g (about 1 cup) granulated sugar
- 4 large eggs
- Zest of 1 lemon
- 1/2 teaspoon almond extract (optional)
- Powdered sugar, for dusting

Instructions:

1. Preheat your oven to 180°C (about 350°F). Grease and flour a round cake pan or springform pan (about 8 inches in diameter).
2. In a mixing bowl, combine the ground almonds and granulated sugar.
3. Separate the egg yolks from the egg whites. In a separate bowl, beat the egg whites until stiff peaks form.
4. Add the egg yolks to the almond-sugar mixture, along with the lemon zest and almond extract (if using). Mix until well combined.
5. Gently fold the beaten egg whites into the almond mixture until just combined. Be careful not to deflate the egg whites too much.
6. Pour the batter into the prepared cake pan, spreading it out evenly.
7. Bake in the preheated oven for 25-30 minutes, or until the cake is golden brown on top and a toothpick inserted into the center comes out clean.
8. Remove the cake from the oven and let it cool in the pan for a few minutes before transferring it to a wire rack to cool completely.
9. Once cooled, dust the top of the cake with powdered sugar.
10. Slice and serve the Gató Mallorquín at room temperature. Optionally, serve with a dollop of whipped cream or a scoop of vanilla ice cream.

Enjoy your delicious Mallorcan Almond Cake!

www.ingramcontent.com/pod-product-compliance
Lightning Source LLC
LaVergne TN
LVHW061942070526
838199LV00060B/3933